soup days.

Dedication

TO DIANE WITH LOVE

Note from the Author:

You might wonder why I put together this book, when the majority of my publications are fictional novels and short stories (other than my fundraising and poetry books.)

I'm sharing this collection because I love these recipes! So easy and quick and tasty – and filling. I can get back to my writing even quicker – and my family can warm up a portion when I'm busy writing my lastest novel.

So I'm sharing them with you – and I hope you love them as much as we do! I figured it was an excellent way to start a new year!!

CATHY MCGOUGH

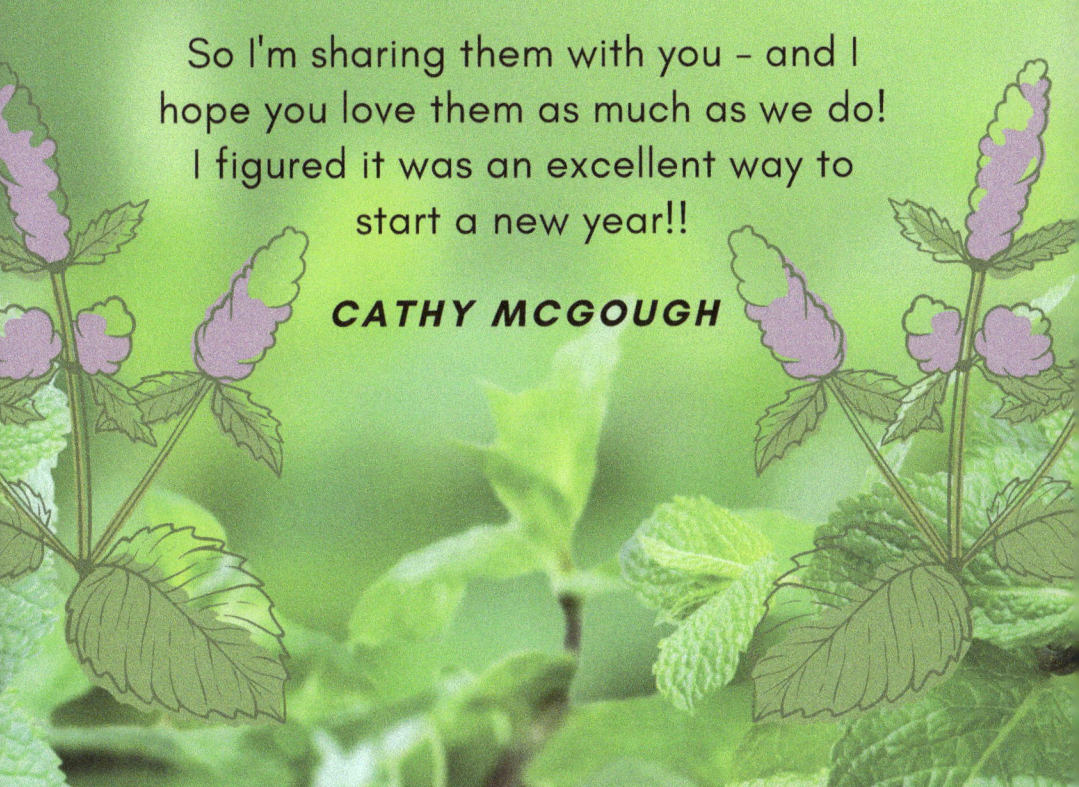

BROCCOLI

Ingredients:

Makes 2x Bowls of Soup.
1 bag of frozen broccoli
500 grams or similar volume
of freshly chopped
1 broth sachet
salt and pepper to taste
soy sauce to taste* optional
milk* optional

To Prepare:

Boil kettle.
Open broth sachet and pour into
measuring cup.
When kettle is boiled, fill up to two cup level.
Open bag of broccoli and pour into sauce
pan big enough to hold contents and the
two cups of hot broth.

BROCCOLI

Stir contents from measuring cup into
pot over broccoli and set to boil.
15 minutes should do it.
Allow to cool on back burner if your blender
does not accommodate hot contents.
Carefully pour contents into your blender
and mix until all the broccoli has been blended.

TASTE TIME

Remove the blender lid and taste.
Add salt, pepper and a splash of soy sauce,
then taste again.
If too thick, add a splash of milk until
the soup is your preferred consistency.
Soup's On - Enjoy!

BROCCOLI

CALORIC
BREAKDOWN

Bag of Frozen Broccoli
(500 grams)
25 calories/85 grams
Chicken sachet 10 calories
salt and pepper to taste 5
calories
*Soy sauce to taste tbsp 8.5
calories
2% milk 1/8 cup 15 calories.
Protein: 3 grams/85 grams
Fibre: 3 grams/85 grams

BROCCOLI

Extras

You can of course add more calories with
Cheddar Cheese
Parmesan Cheese
Croutons
Crackers
Garnishes
Cream instead of milk
Dollop of sour cream -
But you'll find the soup to be very filling
and satisfying as is and if you're counting
calories anytime is soup time!

MUSHROOMS

Ingredients:

Makes 2x Bowls of Soup.

454 grams of mushrooms
1 broth sachet
salt and pepper to taste
soy sauce to taste*
milk.*

To Prepare:

Boil kettle.
Open broth sachet and pour into
measuring cup.
While kettle is boiling slice and clean mushrooms.
When kettle is boiled, fill up to two cup level.
Put cleaned mushrooms and pour into sauce
pan big enough to hold contents and the
two cups of hot broth.

MUSHROOMS

Stir contents from measuring cup into
pot over mushrooms and set to boil.
15 minutes should do it.
Allow to cool on back burner if your blender
does not accommodate hot contents.
Carefully pour contents into your blender
and mix until all the mushrooms have
been blended.

TASTE TIME

Remove the blender lid and taste.
Add salt, pepper and a splash of soy sauce,
then taste again.
If too thick, add a splash of milk until
the soup is your preferred consistency.
Soup's On - Enjoy!

MUSHROOMS

CALORIC BREAKDOWN

454 grams of mushrooms
4 calories/86 grams
Chicken sachet 10 calories
salt and pepper to taste 5 calories
*Soy sauce to taste tbsp 8.5 calories
2% milk 1/8 cup 15 calories.
Protein: .05 x 28 grams
Fibre: .03 grams/28 grams

MUSHROOMS

Extras

You can of course add more calories with:
Cheese
Croutons
Crackers
Garnishes
Oregano
Bay Leaf
Sour Cream
Cream instead of milk -
But you'll find the soup to be very filling
and satisfying as is and if you're counting
calories anytime is soup time!

PEAS

Ingredients:

Makes 4X Bowls of Soup

750 grams of peas
1 broth sachet
salt and pepper to taste
soy sauce to taste*
lime to taste
milk.

To Prepare:

Boil kettle.
Open broth sachet and pour into
measuring cup.
When kettle is boiled, fill up to two cup level.
Pour bag of frozen peas into
pan big enough to hold contents and the
two cups of hot broth.

14

PEAS

Stir contents from measuring cup into
pot over peas and set to boil.
15 minutes should do it.
Allow to cool on back burner if your blender
does not accommodate hot contents.
Carefully pour contents into your blender
and mix until all the peas have
been blended.

TASTE TIME

Remove the blender lid and taste.
Add salt, pepper and a splash of soy sauce,
then taste again.
Add lime and taste.
If too thick, add a splash of milk until
the soup is your preferred consistency- but
careful it doesn't curdle due to the lime.
Soup's On - Enjoy!

PEAS

CALORIC BREAKDOWN

750 grams of peas
70 calories/85 grams
Chicken sachet 10 calories
salt and pepper to taste 5 calories
Lime juice: .5 tbsp. 42 calories
*Soy sauce to taste tbsp 8.5 calories
2% milk 1/8 cup 15 calories.
Protein: 4.6/85 grams
Fibre: 4.2/85 grams

PEAS

Extras

You can of course add more
calories with:
Shredded Cheese
Mint Leaf
Lime Leaf
Bay Leaf
Croutons
Crackers
Garnishes
Sour Cream
Cream instead of milk -
But you'll find the soup to be very
filling and satisfying as is
and if you're counting
calories anytime is soup time!

GIST ONE

Are you getting the gist?

As you've probably figured out, you can use these recipes with any veggies of your choice. You can use fresh or frozen or canned
- whatever is best
for you and your family.

You can also choose which kind of broth sachets or cubes. I use chicken as I prefer it - but if you're veggie use that one. If you like the beef sachet, use that one. If you're making a big batch, combine two different flavours.
It's mix and match.

GIST TWO

BATCHES?

The key to a successful Soup Day is making batches. At first, try a DOUBLE BATCH.

After you blend the first batch, pour into individual containers immediately without lids on.

After cleaning the blender, put in the second batch of soup, blend it, then put immediately into containers and let cool.

TIP: DO NOT ADD milk products at this time. Add it later when you are warming up the soup to serve immediately. This extends the use by date and keep the soup pure until ready to serve and partake in.

TOMATO

Ingredients:

Makes 2X Bowls of Soup

227 grams tomatoes
1 broth sachet
salt and pepper to taste
soy sauce to taste
milk.

To Prepare:

Boil kettle.
Open broth sachet and pour into
measuring cup.
When kettle is boiled, fill up to two cup level.
If you don't like tomato seeds or the skins
you can sift them while you're waiting
for the kettle to boil.
Pour can of tomatoes into
pan big enough to hold contents and the
two cups of hot broth.

TOMATO

Stir contents from measuring cup into
pot over tomatoes and set to boil.
15 minutes should do it.
Allow to cool on back burner if your blender
does not accommodate hot contents.
Carefully pour contents into your blender
and mix until all the tomatoes have
been blended.

TASTE TIME

Remove the blender lid and taste.
Add salt, pepper and a splash of soy sauce,
then taste again.
If too thick, add a splash of milk until
the soup is your preferred consistency- but
careful it doesn't curdle due to the lime.
Soup's On - Enjoy!

TOMATO

CALORIC BREAKDOWN

19 calories/100 grams
Chicken sachet 10 calories
salt and pepper to taste 5 calories
*Soy sauce to taste tbsp 8.5 calories
2% milk 1/8 cup 15 calories.
Protein: 1/100 grams
Fibre: 2/100 grams

TOMATO

Extras

You can of course add more calories with:
Cheddar Cheese
Parmesan Cheese
Croutons
Crackers
Olives
Prawn
Garlic
Basil
Oregano
Cream instead of milk -
But depending on your tastebuds
you'll find the tomato recipe to be
very filling, flavourful and satisfying as is.
Some of the suggestions
above are for healthier items so won't add many
calories. Adding fresh ingredients like spices
to soup is
never a no no!

BUTTERNUT SQUASH

Ingredients:

Makes 2X Bowls of Soup

350 grams butternut squash
1 broth sachet
salt and pepper to taste
soy sauce to taste
milk.

To Prepare:

Boil kettle.
Open broth sachet and pour into
measuring cup.
When kettle is boiled, fill up to two cup level.
Place bag of frozen squash into
pan big enough to hold contents and the
two cups of hot broth.

BUTTERNUT SQUASH

Stir contents from measuring cup into
pot over squash and set to boil.
15 minutes should do it.
Allow to cool on back burner if your blender
does not accommodate hot contents.
Carefully pour contents into your blender
and mix until all the squash has
been blended.

TASTE TIME

Remove the blender lid and taste.
Add salt, pepper and a splash of soy sauce,
then taste again.
If too thick, add a splash of milk until
the soup is your preferred consistency.
Soup's On - Enjoy!

BUTTERNUT SQUASH

CALORIC BREAKDOWN

350 grams of squash
52 calories/100 grams
Chicken sachet 10 calories
salt and pepper to taste 5 calories
*Soy sauce to taste tbsp 8.5 calories
2% milk 1/8 cup 15 calories.
Protein: 1/100 grams
Fibre: 2/100 grams

BUTTERNUT SQUASH

Extras

You can of course add more calories with:
Cheese
Croutons
Crackers
Garnishes
Scallions
Nutmeg
Garlic
Sour Cream
Cream instead of milk -
But depending on your tastebuds
you'll find the squash recipe to be
very filling, flavourful and satisfying as is.
Some of the suggestions
above are for healthier items so won't add many
calories. Adding fresh ingredients like spices
to soup is
never a no no!

POTATO

Ingredients:

Makes 2X Bowls of Soup

1 cup peeled and chopped potatoes
1 broth sachet
salt and pepper to taste
soy sauce to taste
milk or water.

To Prepare:

Boil kettle.
Open broth sachet and pour into
measuring cup.
Clean then peel potatoes and cut into pieces.
When kettle is boiled, fill up to two cup level.
Place potatoes into
pan big enough to hold contents and the
two cups of hot broth.

POTATO

Stir contents from measuring cup into
pot over potatoes and set to boil.
15 or 20 minutes should do it (depends upon
the size of cubes. Note: if very thick add water
to prevent blender from clogging up.
Allow to cool on back burner if your blender
does not accommodate hot contents.
Carefully pour contents into your blender
and mix until all the potatoes have
been blended.

TASTE TIME

Remove the blender lid and taste.
Add salt, pepper and a splash of soy sauce,
then taste again.
If too thick, add a splash of milk or water until
the soup is your preferred consistency.
Soup's On - Enjoy!

POTATO

CALORIC BREAKDOWN

2 cups (279 grams) of chopped potatoes
77 calories/100 grams
Chicken sachet 10 calories
salt and pepper to taste 5 calories
*Soy sauce to taste tbsp 8.5 calories
2% milk 1/8 cup 15 calories.
Protein: 2.02/100 grams
Fibre: 2.2/100 grams

POTATO

Extras

You can of course add more calories with:
Cheddar Cheese
Crumbled Bacon
Ham
Croutons
Crackers
Garlic
Basil
Sour Cream -
But depending on your tastebuds
you'll find the potato recipe to be
very filling, flavourful and satisfying as is.
Some of the suggestions
above are for healthier items so won't add many
calories. Adding fresh ingredients like spices
to soup is
never a no no!

SPINACH

Ingredients:

Makes 2X Bowls of Soup

500 gram bag of frozen spinach
1 broth sachet
1 tbsp. lemon juice (or to taste)
salt and pepper to taste
soy sauce to taste
milk.

To Prepare:

Boil kettle.
Open broth sachet and pour into
measuring cup.
When kettle is boiled, fill up to two cup level.
Place spinach and lemon juice into
pan big enough to hold contents and the
two cups of hot broth.

SPINACH

Stir contents from measuring cup into
pot over spinach and set to boil.
15 minutes should do it.
Allow to cool on back burner if your blender
does not accommodate hot contents.
Carefully pour contents into your blender
and mix until all the spinach has
been blended.

TASTE TIME

Remove the blender lid and taste.
Add salt, pepper and a splash of soy sauce,
then taste again. If too thick, add a splash
of milk or water until the soup is
your preferred consistency. If adding
milk be careful the lemon juice doesn't
cause it to curdle
Soup's On - Enjoy!

SPINACH

CALORIC
BREAKDOWN

500 grams of spinach
23 calories/100 grams
Chicken sachet 10 calories
salt and pepper to taste 5
calories
1 tbsp. lemon juice 29 calories
*Soy sauce to taste tbsp 8.5
calories
2% milk 1/8 cup 15 calories.
Protein: 3/100 grams
Fibre: 2.4/100 grams

SPINACH

Extras

You can of course add more calories with:
Cheddar Cheese
Parmesan
Parsley
Lime Leaf
Croutons
Crackers
Garlic
Basil
Bay Leaf
Sour Cream -
But depending on your tastebuds
you'll find the spinach recipe to be
very filling, flavourful and satisfying as is.
Some of the suggestionsabove are for
healthier items so won't add many calories.
Adding fresh ingredients like spices
to soup is
never a no no!

CORN

Ingredients:

Makes 4X Bowls of Soup

750 gram bag of frozen corn & jalapeno
(any frozen corn will do but this is
my favourite)
2x broth sachets
1 tbsp. butter (optional)
salt and pepper to taste
soy sauce to taste
milk.

To Prepare:

Boil kettle.
Open broth sachets and pour into
measuring cup.
When kettle is boiled, fill up to two cup level.
Place corn and butter into
pan big enough to hold contents and the
two cups of hot broth.

CORN

Stir contents from measuring cup into
pot over corn and set to boil.
15 minutes should do it.
Allow to cool on back burner if your blender
does not accommodate hot contents.
Carefully pour contents into your blender
and mix until all the corn has
been blended.

TASTE TIME

Remove the blender lid and taste.
Add salt, pepper and a splash of soy sauce,
then taste again.
If too thick, add a splash of milk or water until
the soup is your preferred consistency.
Soup's On - Enjoy!

CORN

CALORIC BREAKDOWN

750 grams of corn
96 calories/100 grams
Chicken sachet 10 calories
salt and pepper to taste 5
calories
1 tbsp. butter 102 calories
(optional)
*Soy sauce to taste tbsp 8.5
calories
2% milk 1/8 cup 15 calories.
Protein: 3.4/100 grams
Fibre: 2.4/100 grams

CORN

Extras

You can of course add more calories with:
Parsley
Croutons
Crackers
Garlic Butter
Basil
Bay Leaf
Chili flakes
Sour Cream -
But depending on your tastebuds
you'll find the corn recipe to be
very filling, flavourful and satisfying as is.
Some of the suggestions
above are for healthier items so won't add many
calories. Adding fresh ingredients like spices
to soup is
never a no no!

BULK SOUPING

ARE YOU READY
FOR ALL FOUR BURNERS
ON THE GO?

When you're ready it's time to branch out and begin making larger batches of soups all in one go.

Choose the family favourites, do a big shop - and get cooking!

Make sure you have plenty of storage containers on hand. Since the recipes include frozen veggies, it's not advisable to refreeze them.

Once your entire family knows that your soup is always readily available - then it'll be a popular go to as a low calorie, nutrious snacking option.

Imagine all the free time you'll have!

ASPARAGUS

Ingredients:

Makes 2X Bowls of Soup

340 gram bag of frozen asparagus
1 broth sachet
1 tbsp. butter (optional)
salt and pepper to taste
soy sauce to taste
milk.

To Prepare:

Boil kettle.
Open broth sachet and pour into
measuring cup.
When kettle is boiled, fill up to two cup level.
Place asparagus into
pan big enough to hold contents and the
two cups of hot broth.

ASPARAGUS

Stir contents from measuring cup into
pot over asparagus and set to boil.
15 minutes should do it.
Allow to cool on back burner if your blender
does not accommodate hot contents.
Carefully pour contents into your blender
and mix until all the corn has
been blended.

TASTE TIME

Remove the blender lid and taste.
Add salt, pepper and a splash of soy sauce,
then taste again.
If too thick, add a splash of milk or water until
the soup is your preferred consistency.
Soup's On - Enjoy!

ASPARAGUS

CALORIC
BREAKDOWN

340 grams of asparagus
50 calories/86 grams
Chicken sachet 10 calories
salt and pepper to taste 5
calories
*Soy sauce to taste tbsp 8.5
calories
2% milk 1/8 cup 15 calories.
Protein: 2/86 grams
Fibre: 1/86 grams

ASPARAGUS

Extras

You can of course add more calories with:
Parsley
Croutons
Crackers
Fresh asparagus
Garlic Butter
Basil
Bay Leaf
Bacon bits
Butter
But depending on your tastebuds
you'll find the asparagus recipe to be
very filling, flavourful and satisfying as is.
Some of the suggestions
above are for healthier items
so won't add many
calories. Adding fresh ingredients like
spices
to soup is
never a no no!

ONION

Ingredients:

Makes 2X Bowls of Soup

283 grams bag of frozen onions
1 broth sachet
sherry or red wine (optional)
salt and pepper to taste
soy sauce to taste
milk.

To Prepare:

Boil kettle.
Open broth sachet and pour into
measuring cup.
When kettle is boiled, fill up to two cup level.
Place onions (and wine or sherry if desired)
pan big enough to hold contents and the
two cups of hot broth.

ONION

Stir contents from measuring cup into
pot over onions set to boil.
15 minutes should do it.
If you prefer some onion pieces intact,
remove them and place them into a bowl
before blending.
Allow to cool on back burner if your blender
does not accommodate hot contents.
Carefully pour contents into your blender
and mix until all the corn has
been blended.

TASTE TIME

Remove the blender lid and taste.
Add salt, pepper and a splash of soy sauce,
then taste again.
If too thick, add a splash of milk or water until
the soup is your preferred consistency.
Soup's On - Enjoy!

ONION

CALORIC BREAKDOWN

283 grams of onion
30 calories/85 grams
Chicken sachet 10 calories
salt and pepper to taste 5
calories
*Soy sauce to taste tbsp 8.5
calories
2% milk 1/8 cup 15 calories.
Protein: 1.1/100 grams
Fibre: 1.7/100 grams

ONION

Extras

You can of course add more calories with:
Cheese
Wine or Sherry
Egg
Parsley
Croutons
Crackers
Butter.
But depending on your tastebuds
you'll find the onion recipe to be
very filling, flavourful and satisfying as is.
Some of the suggestions
above are for healthier items so won't add many
calories. Adding fresh ingredients like spices
to soup is
never a no no!

SOUP
DAYS

Ideas to try

CAULIFLOWER
BRUSSEL SPROUTS
CHICK PEAS (with Garam Masala)
KIDNEY BEANS
CAPSICUM (PEPPERS)
AVOCADO
CUCUMBERS
CELERY
KALE
SWEET POTATOES
CABBAGE
Add FISH or PRAWNS
Add CHICKEN or BEEF

SOUP
DAYS

The sky is the limit with these versatile
recipes and there's a lot of room for
experimentation...
Have fun - and don't be afraid to
mix and match!

I've given you my favourite recipes.
If I included all the soups I've made
the price of my book would get too
expensive!

ABOUT THE AUTHOR:

Multi-award-winning author,
Cathy McGough
lives and writes in Oakville, Ontario,
Canada with her husband, son and two cats.
If you'd like to get in touch with Cathy,
you can send her an email:

cathy@cathymcgough.com.

Cathy loves to hear from her readers!